To my parents...

They taught me that asking correct questions precedes finding the correct answers. This concept was the start of the Taxes Mastered system.

To my wife...

Thank you for your support that makes my professional life possible and my entire life joyful.

To the Taxes Mastered Community...

Thank you for allowing us to be part of your team. It is exciting to team with a client community energetically striving to smartly achieve their goals on-time, on-budget, and with the highest probability of success.

To the Team at Taxes Mastered...

Using the tax code as an authoritarian standard, you are truly helping clients achieve their goals. Achievement brings a strong and proper sense of purpose and dignity to their lives. Thank you for caring so much about our clients and so much about the process.

Table of Contents

Friendly Word of Advice… iii
Chapter 1: From Being Dismissive to Believing 1
Chapter 2: Who Should Read This Book? 6
Chapter 3: You Pay Too Much Tax by Ignoring the Purpose of the Tax Code 9
Chapter 4: You Pay Too Much In Tax When You Look For Help From the Wrong School 16
Chapter 5: You Pay Too Much In Tax When Goals and Taxing Models Are Not Aligned 32
    Addendum Number 1: ERISA Plans 43
    Addendum Number 2: Non-qualified Plans (NQPs) ... 51
Chapter 6: You Pay Too Much In Tax When You Drive Risk from Reasonable to Beyond 65
Chapter 7: You Pay Too Much In Tax When You Do Not Know Your End Game 78
Chapter 8: An Easy Way to Know if You Pay Too Much in Taxes 82
Chapter 9: Definitions 85
Disclosures and Disclaimers 89
About the Author .... Error! Bookmark not defined.

Friendly Word of Advice...

Taxes Mastered, Inc. uses a proprietary system based on my research. This research began in the early 1980s and continues beyond the date of writing of this book.

This system is based on the authoritarian standards and on the achievement paths develop by the Internal Revenue Code of 1986 (tax code), and is based on thousands upon thousands of interactions with clients, the Team at Taxes Mastered, the team of my historical certified public accountant (CPA) firm, the team of my other business activities, non-team tax professionals such as CPAs and Enrolled Agents (EAs), and non-team financial advisors.

To ensure clients properly receive this system, I developed and enforce an on-going certification process. This process begins before a person is considered a member of the Taxes Mastered Team and continues throughout their association with the Team. The certification process and internal reviews ensures the client that the education, analysis, recommendations, and paths of implementation offered by a team member are in full harmony with the system and are provided by qualified and dedicated Team professionals.

To ensure clients properly receive this system, each Team Member is, in turn, part of a larger Team. At Taxes Mastered, a Team Member does not make recommendations in isolation; recommendations reflect the considered judgement of their larger Team.

Only properly certified Team members:

- ✓ Have the full scope, vision, and authoritarian positions of support of this book.
- ✓ Have the skills, knowledge, and judgement to successfully implement its concept for you.
- ✓ Have the needed support of other properly certified Team members to successfully implement its concepts for you.

My advice to the reader of this book is NOT TO IMPLEMENT strategies discussed in this book unless those strategies were developed and fully implemented by a certified Taxes Mastered Team Member in association with their larger Team.

To locate a Team Member in your area, please contact us through our website at www.TaxesMastered.com.

One final note… it might seem that this book is nothing more than a sales pitch for Taxes Mastered, Inc. If that is your impression after reading the book and taking the assessment, then I am sorry you did not gain a true understanding for what I am trying to achieve with this book.

I strongly believe Taxes Mastered is on the forefront and is a major thought leader for restoring to small business owners what they absolutely need in strategic tax services; services that are generally not available today for the market addressed in this book.

I strongly believe that every small business owner, as defined in this book, would greatly benefit from the services provided by Taxes Mastered. However, if they do not receive their absolutely needed services from Taxes Mastered, at the least they will know what they need and can be intelligent shoppers in the marketplace.

Chapter 1: From Being Dismissive to Believing

Summary

- ✓ 85%+ of all small business owners pay too much in tax.
- ✓ A primary reason for this 85%+ percentage is they and their tax professionals think the primary purpose of the tax code is to raise money for the government. This is not true.
- ✓ The primary purpose of the tax code is to help taxpayers achieve their goals on-time, on-budget, and with the highest probability of success.
- ✓ By not understanding the primary purpose of the tax code, taxpayers cut themselves off from substantial tax benefits and savings, and pay too much in tax.

Expanded discussion

85%+ of all small business owners pay too much in tax.

I make this supportable statement based on my research conducted since the mid-1980s. How did I come to recognize this percentage?

The 85%+ number was recognized as I began to listen to my clients, to develop the analytical models to "prove they were right even though they intuitively knew they were right", and to find the proper system for removing them from the 85%+ category.

My professional journey began being dismissive with my clients.

In the mid-1980s, I operated a CPA firm in the Phoenix, Arizona area. I launched this CPA firm on 1 July 1979 and was busy trying to learn how to be a CPA to small businesses as well as trying to learn how to be a small business owner. I would visit with my clients or clients interviewing me to become their CPA, and almost all of them would say they paid too much in tax. Instead of agreeing with them, which would have been the right answer, I was dismissive of them. I thought it was equivalent to them saying it was hot in Phoenix in July. Yes, but it is what it is and, besides, it is not going to snow (change) so live with it.

I also thought the comment from small business owners that they paid too much in tax had a firm basis in the "kill the messenger" mentality.

In those days I thought the primary purpose of the tax code was to raise money for the government. As my clients did not want to give money to the government and wanted to use it for themselves, there was bound to be a natural tension which was expressed in the statement that "I pay too much in tax."

But the small business owner side of my education clicked in and asked why I was not listening to my market. I began to ask myself why such a large portion of the market thought they were paying too much in tax when the vast majority of tax professionals were simply dismissive.

My professional journey traveled to believing them but not knowing why.

I started on a search to find out if they were correct. I conducted in-depth studies of my clients and clients interviewing me to become their CPA, gathered client stories about taxes, subjected these stories to mathematical analysis, and subjected these stories to the authoritarian standards of the tax code. Why the tax code?

In much of our lives, opinion is viewed as fact. Especially in the financial area, opinions about the direction of the market, for example, takes on the aura of fact. I did not want my client's subjected to my opinion. The tax code is the authoritarian standard applicable to taxes. Violations of the tax code can result in money being taken away as penalties, fines, interest, and other charges. More serious violations can result in the loss of economic-producing assets. Even more serious violations can result in jail or prison time. This makes the tax code an authoritarian standard.

My clients did not want opinions, they wanted facts; the tax code provided those facts. But the facts were blurred by my perception (and, in fact, the perception of the clients) that the purpose of the tax code was to raise money for the government. As long as that perception remained, I was not going to find out why my clients were paying too much in taxes.

My professional journey matured into understanding why.

Before I understood why, I researched the tax code much like an adversarial adventure looking for the loopholes in the tax code that would give my clients the edge…the edge to reduce their tax load. Therefore, I adopted an us versus them mentality. This mentality was fatal to finding the answer.

One day, in the mid-1980s, while I was studying the tax code, I had a major break-out thought that my perception of the tax code was completely wrong. I thought the primary purpose of the tax code was to raise money for the government. This thought was wrong. The primary purpose of the tax code is to help people achieve their goals on-time, on-budget, and with the highest probability of success.

Let me repeat that break-out thought again: The primary purpose of the tax code is to help people achieve their goals on-time, on-budget, and with the highest probability of success.

Once I understood that, the answer to why my clients, in fact 85%+ of all small business owners, were paying too much in tax was because I, as the tax professional, was not using the tax code to their advantage. The tax code wanted to help but I refused that help by viewing the tax code as an adversary.

How wrong I was and how negatively it affected the clients.

When I began to utilize that break-out thought that the tax code was a help to my clients, I began to see the tax benefits and savings offered by the tax code. I also understood that the term *tax savings* was not just what the client could save on their current year's tax return. I saw that the term *tax savings* covered three divisions of time:

- Taxes generated from the current year's tax return.
- Taxes generated from economic growth from today forward.
- Taxes generated from the use of economic resources from today forward.

As I interfaced with tax professionals through books, seminars, shared work on clients, and other points of contact, at times they challenge my statement that 85%+ of all small business owners pay too much in tax. They offer various academic arguments based on self-created case studies. Academic arguments are not the focus of this book.

Very rarely does a small business owner challenge that statement; they intuitively know they pay too much in tax but do not know where to turn for help.

What works in the real world is the purpose of this book.

Therefore, this challenge is offered:

> *Challenge: Have one of your clients take the assessment explained in* Is There an Easy Way to See If I Pay Too Much in Taxes? *If the assessment results show your clients are paying too much in taxes, allow Taxes Mastered, Inc. to review their filed tax returns. If the assessment shows they pay too much in tax, our review should document substantial areas for tax savings.*
>
> *If Taxes Mastered cannot show substantial tax savings, then my claim of the 85%+ result should be viewed as suspect in their case.*
>
> *If Taxes Mastered can show substantial tax savings, then my claim of the 85%+result should be viewed as correct in their case.*

Chapter 2: Who Should Read This Book?

Summary

- ✓ This is not a one-size-fits-all book.
- ✓ This book was written for a clearly defined small business owner.
- ✓ This book is written so you can know why you pay too much in tax.

Expanded discussion

This book is not a one-size-fits-all; it is written for a very specific client.

- You are a small business owner (SBO).
- Your business has been successful since inception (good years outweigh bad years).
- You have under $90 million in gross annual revenue.
- Your profit is usually equal to or greater than 5% of gross annual revenue.
- You have fewer than 100 (+/-) employees.
- Your business is owned between 6 or less active owners.
- Your business's principal product or service is not important.
- Your business's tax filing form (1040, 1120, 1120-S, or 1065) is not important.
- Your business's legal structure (sole proprietorship, partnership, corporation, or LLC) is not important.
- Your business's location of operation is not important.

If you do not fit that client profile, then the book's influence is diminished. This diminishment occurs as the tax code develops safe paths for achievement based on, for example, business's revenue size, number of employees, and other factors. There is a real danger in providing tax services when the tax professional sees all clients as really the same, really needing the same service, and really needing a standardized approached. This is not the approach of the tax code and it is not the approach of this book.

This book is written so you can know why you pay too much in tax. This book is written to explain what paying too much in taxes really means: it means your quest for achievement of your goals will take longer to accomplish, take more resources, and, in fact, significantly lowers the probability of you even reaching your stated goals.

This book is written to explain why the 85%+ number is correct and how you can begin to fully utilize the tax code to reach your goals on-time, on-budget, and with the highest probability of success.

Key definitions are provided so you and I will have an agreement on what specific terms mean.

By now, you have probably noticed this book is written in the first-person and that *I* is often used. This is done on purpose as I want this book to act as a conversation between us. Therefore, this book has a very personalized tone.

This book and the Taxes Mastered System could be the difference between:

- Achieving your goals on-time, on-budget, and with the highest probability of success by following the safe and prudent paths (and receiving the intended tax benefits) established by the tax code

- Lowering your achievement standards, taking longer to reach these lowered standards, and facing an increasing probability of failure (not reaching them at all).

You only have an overly-burdensome tax load to lose.

Chapter 3: You Pay Too Much Tax by Ignoring the Purpose of the Tax Code

Summary

- The primary purpose of the tax code is to help you achieve specific goals supported by the tax code.
- A secondary, and maybe tertiary, purpose is to raise money for the government.
- The process of aligning your goals to tax code-supported goals is achieved through social engineering.
- The tax code helps you achieve by granting substantial tax benefits.
- You pay too much in tax when
    - You do not know the primary purpose of the tax code.
    - You do not align your goals with the primary purpose of the tax code

Expanded discussion

I write books, teach seminars, prepare continuing professional education (CPE) material for CPAs, and in other ways interface with tax professionals outside of my Teams at Taxes Mastered. When I am with non-Team tax professionals, I often ask them this question: **What is the purpose of the tax code?**

The overwhelming response they provide is the purpose of the tax code is to raise money for the government. The second response, offered less often but still quite frequently, is to raise money for the government but offer very limited loopholes that cannot and will not benefit my clients. Clearly, these non-team professionals view the tax code in an adversarial manner with their job being to squeeze as much as possible from the enemy for their clients.

No wonder 85%+ of small businesses pay too much in tax!

Both of these answers are wrong and have been wrong since the 1930s.

If the primary purpose of the tax code is to raise money for the government with or without limited applicable loopholes, then why does the tax code, time and time again, forgo tax revenue for a higher social purpose?

If the primary purpose of the tax code is to raise money for the government, then with all relevant factors being the same, why…

- Does a single person pay more than a married couple?
- Does a married couple with no children pay more tax than a married couple with children?
- Does a married couple with children living in an apartment pay more than a married couple with children living in a mortgaged home?

The answer to the question of **Why?** is the social purpose of the tax code favors a married couple with children living in their own home over all other family relationships and offers substantial tax benefits for complying taxpayers. This is the answer, like it or not. Like it or not, the tax code deeply engages in the concept of social engineering.

As *Chapter 5: You Pay too Much In Taxes When Goals and Taxing Models are Not Aligned* explains, the philosophy of social engineering and the granting of substantial tax benefits for taxpayers aligning their personal goals with the goals engineered by the tax code are deeply embedded inside the tax code.

You pay too much in tax when you do not know the primary purpose of the tax code and you pay too much in tax when you do not align your personal goals with the primary purpose of the tax code.

The following history of the tax code is adopted from a chapter of a continuing professional education class (CPE) for CPAs on maximizing distributions from an ERISA plan like a 401(k) plan that I wrote. This chapter explains why the purpose of the tax code was changed in the mid-1930s from generating revenue for the government to social engineering. Another name for social engineering is developing safe and prudent paths within the tax code so complying taxpayers could receive substantial tax benefits to achieve their goals on-time, on-budget, and with the highest probability of success.

> *This chapter documents how Congress changed the primary purpose of the Internal Revenue Code during the New Deal era and then used that changed purpose decades later to create the two polar-opposite distributive options.*
>
> ### *History*
>
> *Historically, the purpose of the Internal Revenue Code was revenue production through taxation. The Internal Revenue Code produced tax revenue by taxing a wide range of economic transactions and by taxing those transactions on a progressive theory.*

The progressive theory is a philosophy that bands taxable income into ranges with each increasing range taxed at a higher rate per taxable dollar than the previous range. As an example, for the tax year ended 2014, the Tax Foundation documented that for married couples filing jointly, the band from $18,151 to $73,800 was taxed at 15% while the band from $226,851 to $405,100 was taxed at 28%. Revenue production was the justification for the existence and voluntary acceptance of the Internal Revenue Code. This historical arrangement was operable until President Franklin Roosevelt and his New Deal.

The New Deal came in two parts and was a series of federal legislations designed to offset the economic and social conditions of the early 1930s commonly referred to as the Great Depression. President Roosevelt's New Deal focused on relief for the unemployed and the poor, recovery of the economy to normal levels, and reform of the financial system to prevent a repeat of the Great Depression. The first part of the New Deal came in 1933 and 1934, and the second part in 1935 through 1938. Although this conclusion is very controversial, many economists then and now believe that without the New Deal, the Great Depression would had continued longer and had more serious results. A far less controversial statement is that the New Deal changed the economic, political, and tax code landscape of the country.

While President Roosevelt was concerned about raising the money needed to implement the New Deal, his greater concern was maintaining his momentous changes. President Roosevelt introduced sweeping and dramatic changes in the social landscape with his New Deal. He believed pure emotion (voter acceptance today) might not sustain the changes going forward, especially through the adjustments required. He worried that, over time, the New Deal would collapse and his vision for changes in America would be lost. He determined to cement his vision for the future by using the Internal Revenue Code to encourage or discourage certain social behaviors from the citizens, in line with the stated purposes of the New Deal. Cementing his vision within the Internal Revenue Code required a change from its historical purpose of revenue production through taxation to a new purpose of incentivizing taxpayers to accept and engage in the social change of the New Deal. This process of incentivizing taxpayers is social engineering.

Social Engineering

Social engineering looks backward from the finish to the start. It starts with goals or social purposes in mind and then completes actions required to achieve those goals and social purposes. Social engineering is like starting a maze at the end and working backward to the start. Congress started with the social engineered results needed for the New Deal and then created legislation through the Internal Revenue Code to make those results happen. Social engineering uses the Internal Revenue Code as an economic incentive for taxpayers to do what the government desires. To motivate the taxpayer–citizen to accept and engage in its goals and social purposes, the government offers an economic incentive through lower taxes for taxpayers acting in accordance with its goals or purposes.

> *Author's comment: Examples of social engineering are throughout the Internal Revenue Code. As an example, the government wished to encourage home ownership. Therefore, there is a deduction for interest paid on a home mortgage and a deduction for property taxes paid on the home. The government did not want to encourage renting of a home and, therefore, these deductions are not available to a renter.*
>
> *Another example is the government wished to encourage marriage with children. The progressive tax rates for a married couple are lower than the progressive tax rates for a single taxpayer. Married couples with children pay an even lower progressive tax, since they can deduct an amount based on the number of children. Married taxpayers with children have additional tax incentives not offered to married couples without children or single taxpayers.*

President Roosevelt felt that citizens would change their personal behaviors to receive the economic incentive through lower taxes, even if they were not fully committed to the philosophy of the change. If the citizens did not change to the desired behavior, there was an economic penalty charged in the form of higher taxes. The changes in the Internal Revenue Code promoting social engineering had the potential to become permanent legislation, meaning any changes would ordinarily be incremental and not designed to alter the original purpose of the legislation. With this permanent cementing of his vision of the future, President Roosevelt moved acceptance of the New Deal from philosophical agreement to people acting in their best economic interests (choosing directly to save taxes and indirectly, therefore, accepting the related social behavior) rather than acting by pure emotion or commitment to a vision.

With the understanding that the primary purpose of the tax code is building safe and prudent paths offering substantial tax benefits to assist taxpayers in achieving shared goals on-time, on-budget, and with the highest probability of success, you can now:

- Use the tax code to your benefit.
- See the tax code as a help...almost as a member of your team...in achieving your goals.
- See the tax code as an aid to building safe and prudent paths for your business as you achieve your goals.
- See that there is more to the tax code than preparing your tax return, weighting you down, slowing your process, lowering the probability of your achievement, requiring more time and resources as you try and achieve your goals, and leaving you with an overly burdensome tax load.

Chapter 4: You Pay Too Much In Tax When You Look For Help From the Wrong School

Summary
- Pre-early 1990s, the right place to look for tax help was the CPA or EA.
- Post-early 1990s, things changed and, in my opinion, the tax help given earlier was not generally available to the small business owner as defined in this book.
- The dominate tax service provided post early-1990s is tax return preparation (tactical).
- You pay too much in tax when focus on tactical and basically ignore strategic tax services.
- Today, the small business owner is looking for someone to help them ACCOMPLISH THEIR GOALS; all they are getting is someone telling them WHAT THEY DID.

Expanded discussion

Where do you go for help with taxes? My obvious answer would be to go to a tax professional for help with taxes. In my opinion, the tax professional should:
- ✓ Care deeply about the client.
- ✓ Help the client achieve their goals.
- ✓ Use the tax code and its tax benefits to help the client.
- ✓ Take a long-term focus.
- ✓ Be there with the client throughout the current tax year and beyond into tomorrow.
- ✓ Have a relatively small percentage of their total revenue come from tax preparation.

Was the obvious answer ever correct? There are three schools of thought on tax services with widely differing focuses as shown in Table 1

Table 1: Three Different Schools on Providing Tax Services

Characteristics	Old School: Strategic and Tactical	New School: Fractional Service focused on tactical	Taxes Mastered School: Strategic plus tactical oversight
Level of professional interaction	Very high	Moderate to low	Very high
Focus	Strategy and tactical	Tactical	Strategy
Roles	Generals, sergeants, and messengers	Messengers	Generals and sergeants
Time horizon	Today, tomorrow and in the future	Today with minor emphasis on tomorrow	Today, tomorrow and in the future
Use of tax code	To achieve goals of clients	To prepare tax returns	To achieve goals of clients
Emphasis on tax return	By-product of proper strategic planning	Primary emphasis	By-product of proper strategic planning
"What if" scenarios	Naturally occurring	Seldom prepared as strategy is not a focus	Naturally occurring
Delivered by	CPAs and EAs	CPAs, EAs, and part-time labor	Appropriate professionals as multi-disciplines needed
Use of technology	Limited	High	High
Benefit to taxpayer	Achieve their goals on-time, on-budget, and with the highest probability of success	Tax returns filed	Achieve their goals on-time, on-budget, and with the highest probability of success
Current status	Mostly abandoned by early 1990s	Predominate model for tax services	Limited geographical availability but rapidly growing

With a background as a CPA starting in the mid-1970s, I have a very strong affinity for the Old School: Full Service model. I understand the inherent problems with that model but I also understand that these problems did not deter the CPA and the EA from delivering a high value product commensurate with the price charged for the small business owner and focusing on the needs and the goals of the small business owner.

> *In my opinion:* As a small business owner, I much prefer having someone ask me what I am trying to accomplish; second choice is asking what I did. In the area of taxes, asking me my goals is critical to achieving my goals; it is nearly fatal to achieving my goals if their first question is asking me what I did.
>
> **Tax preparers today as what I did...I need to have them ask me what I am trying to do.**

However, this affinity is not "for the good old days" but rather affinity for a model that worked very well for the small business owner, and affinity for a model that is truly needed today.

The following is a discussion of certain key characteristics of the Old School, New School, and the Taxes Mastered School. For this book, *strategy* or *strategic* is the development of a plan of action towards the achievement of a specific and workable goal; achievement defined within a specific time period.

The plan must be supportable by adherence to the authoritarian standard of the tax code.

For the purpose of this book, *tactical* is the implementation of the strategy. The main tactical activity for the tax professionals of today is preparing a tax return.

Old School: Full strategic and tactical tax services focused on goal achievement

The Old School model arose in a time where **high level of personal interaction** in commercial transactions was common. Part of the reason for the high level of personal interaction was the social culture of the times. Part of it was the lack of computer and communication technology which necessitated face-to-face dialogue to conduct business. Part of it was the localized nature of commerce where small businesses served their neighbors by offering products very customized to fit needs of clients. And part of it was clients saw and understood the economic benefit in the of full service tax model

The **focus** of commerce was helping neighbors achieve their goals. The primary focus and delivery mode for commerce was the neighborhood small business owner. Tax service firms reflected that primary focus as they were involved in strategic and tactical activities for the neighborhood small business owner and, generally, were a small neighborhood business themselves.

The **roles** played by the tax professionals were generals, sergeants, and messengers.

Generals as historically CPAs and EAs were core providers of strategic and tactical tax services. They developed strategies to win the war…achieve the goals…of the client. As generals, they could look over the entire field of play and understand all the parts, how those parts should work together, and how those parts needed to work together.

Sergeants as historically CPAs and EAs actively assisted with implementation of those strategies. The Old School

CPAs and EAs were in the "battle" with their clients helping them adopt, adapt, and achieve. They were sergeants as they provided a degree of comfort based on competency.

Messengers as they reported on the success of those strategies and tactical decisions by preparing a final report (for the purposes of our discussion) called the tax return. While they also prepared financial statements, the tax return was the final report for the year provided to the government based on the authoritarian standards of the tax code.

As generals, sergeants, and messengers the CPAs and the EAs **time horizon** for service was before, during, and beyond the current tax year. They started their service for the current tax year in the year preceding. This allowed for planning to form an operational model for the year.

They stayed with the operational model during the year. This allowed them to be part of the proactive response to changes that occurred from the anticipated operational model. They reported on the results of the current year. Part of the reporting was to the government by filing tax forms. Part of the reporting was to management so continually improving models could be built.

The Old School CPAs and EAs used the **tax code** in accordance with its primary purpose. The primary purpose of the tax code since the mid-1930s is to help taxpayers achieve their goals by offering substantial tax benefits. For further discussion, see the *Chapter 3: You Pay Too Much in Taxes by Ignoring the Purpose of the Tax Code.* They did not think the primary purpose of the tax code was to raise money for the government.

The CPAs and EAs of the Old School understood the **emphasis on the tax return** was a by-product of their total operational influence. The tax return was, at best, secondary, and never of primary importance.

A product of the full service the CPAs and the EAs provided were **"What-If scenarios"**; these were produced as a natural by-product of their full service. As they were actively involved with the small business's management team, the use of "What-Ifs" was a natural by-product of their service. As reality unfolded and was gauged against the operational model, reality needed to be reflected. Estimates of the trends and results of reality naturally produced "What-Ifs" as a means of verifying the underlying validity of the operational model and to predict what could happen currently and in the future if various decisions were made.

In the Old School model, **tax services were delivered by CPAs and EAs** who made a firm commitment to extensive formal educational training before they were allowed to serve the public, firm commitment to continuing professional education during their span of service, and a firm commitment to a demanding professional code of ethics. Tax services were delivered by trained and government licensed tax professionals. Tax professionals were held accountable for their performance and conduct financially and by the threat of a loss of license in cases of material professional neglect of duties.

In the Old School, **technology was limited**. Part of the lack of extensive technology during the years of the Old School was the extent of computer and communication development at the time. Part of it was the tenor of the culture at the time which demanded that the CPAs and EAs be adoptive to the on-going relationship with the client.

Technology is wonderful in its proper role. However, no computer program yet developed can adapt the tax code to the needs of a client and the achievement of their goals as well as the reasoned, experienced, and prudent mind of a diligent tax professional in a face-to-face, deeply interpersonal relationship with the client.

In my opinion, the summary of the tremendous **benefits to client** from the Old School approach is that they had a total tax team with all needed services being provided. Clients could, and vast numbers did, achieve their goals on-time, on-budget, and with the highest probability of success.

In my opinion, the **current status** of the Old School model is abandonment. In my opinion, this is not the operational model today for most CPAs and EAs providing tax services to the small business owner. This model was mostly abandoned by the early-1990s. By abandonment I mean that while there are isolated cases of CPAs and EAs operating under the Old School model, by and large, the vast majority of tax firms offering services do not comport to this model.

The **reasons for demise** are varied and highly tailored to a specific CPA or EA Firms; however, there are some commonalities:

- The Old School's high personal level of service model became economically harder to sustain with the rise of fractional tax service firms (New School as discussed below).
- The Old School did not adequately explain the worth of a full service model to the marketplace as it began to change.

- The Old School was mostly dismissive and non-responsive to rise of the New School of tax service firms.
- The Old School could not figure out how to use technology to continue full service model at an economically-viable price.

> *In my opinion:* Under the Old School tax approach, the first step was the CPA or EA learning the client goals and using the achievement of those goals as the standard for all economic, personal, and tax decisions. After that first step, the CPA or EA offered their professional tax services. In due time, a tax return was prepared but perhaps months and months after the first step.
>
> Under the New School approach, the first step is for someone (CPA, EA or perhaps not either professional designation) to have the client fill-out a fact form about the year just ended…information provided after the fact. Then, someone performs a data entry function using tax software and a tax return is produced.
>
> How can that approach possibly produce the strategic and tactical tax services needed by the client?

New School: Fractional tactical service focused on the tax return

The New School arose in a time where **low level of personal interaction** in commercial transactions was growing to be common. Part of it was the social culture of the times. Part of it was rise of computer and communication technology which flourished the thought (erroneously in my opinion) that extensive face-to-face dialogue to conduct business was no longer needed. Part of it was trend away for the localized nature of commercial reach. Technology and replication of business models allowed small businesses to serve geographically unconnected areas. Product offerings became more focused and standardized. Tax services focused on preparing tax returns and tax returns became a commodity.

The full service Old School tax firms followed this trend. They moved from their customized and total service business model to a material focus on the tax return as a product. One telling result of this movement is the historical, global relationship between revenue from tax services to revenue from tax return preparation.

The Old School generally had tax return preparation as a low percentage of total tax revenue. The New School has tax return preparation as a very high percentage of total tax revenue. With this change in focus, clients no long saw the economic benefit of the full service model. Quite frankly, this was a foregone conclusion when the very companies providing full service were now offering restricted services.

The New School's **focus** was filing tax returns. Business consultants became the preferred source of consulting on goal achievement. While business consultants play a vital role, their economic cost drove many small business owners away. Small business owners, practically speaking, did not have access to the services offered by the Old School any longer.

With the change in focus by the New School, their **roles** were messengers for the most part. Tax services became predominately focused on providing a tax return and reporting the amount of money owed to the government.

The New School's **time horizon** for service was after the end of the tax year. They started their service for the current tax year after that year had ended. How could they impact the current year when it was over before they provided their services? How could they have much impact on the future years as their services were limited?

The tax code's primary purpose (helping taxpayer's achieve goals) was changed to raising revenue for the government from the filing of tax returns. The **tax code was used** to file tax returns and not help clients achieve their goals on-time, on-budget, and with the highest probability of success. The tax code was used in a fractional nature just as the provided services were fractional in nature.

Under the New School, the **emphasis was on tax return**. The tax return was of primary importance. This emphasis on tax return preparation and not full service is why the New School, in my opinion, offers only fractional service.

Under this fractional approach, **"What-If scenarios"** were mostly abandoned. The New School offered some limited remodeling of the tax return but mostly the software produced comparisons and effects of minor changes in deduction levels. "What-Ifs" became a presentation on deductions and not on goal achievement.

In addition, the New School's fractional service model did not require the services of CPAs and EAs. In the New School, **services could be delivered by part-time labors in addition to CPAs and EAs**. Fractional services allowed for rise of the part-time labor that were not government licensed and were without extensive formal educational training before providing services to clients. In addition, as the service providers were not licensed, continuing professional education became optional and mostly abandoned. (For example, CPAs are required to take 40-hours per year of continuing professional education generally reported over a two-year period.) Labor savings due to seasonal, non-licensed workers preparing tax returns resulted in a lowering of cost of services over full service model. Tax return became a commodity and not a customized, one-off work.

Full service offerings became very costly when compared to the commodity of tax return preparation.

> *In my opinion:* Software developers faced a marketplace problem. If their software-produced returns had an unfavorable audit rate, 5% (+/-) or less when examined by the Internal Revenue Service (IRS), that software might not thrive in the marketplace. Therefore, software developers began to program as the default those options that were most agreeable to the IRS.
>
> While these default options could be changed in the software, it took a tax professional with a deep understanding of the code to do so and these types of preparers were not the norm in the New School.
>
> Therefore, the tax return had the very real potential of producing a higher tax liability than needful.

In the New School, **technology was critical**. Software technology allowed for the programing-in of tax code options so that the full range of options did not have to be known or understood by the tax preparer and could be selected based on a mathematical algorithm. Therefore, years of extensive training was no longer required to "prepare" a tax return. Software allowed part-time seasonal labor to prepare tax returns.

My conclusion: Tax software technology made for very efficient and low cost tax return preparation with returns being produced with options most favorable to the IRS. This technology model was more effective in the individual tax preparation model. It was less effective in the small business tax preparation model.

Individuals filing their personal income tax return (Form 1040) received the greatest lower cost **benefit** of the New School approach. Form 1040s were now being prepared more effectively, efficiently, and at lower cost. Small business owners filing business returns received the greatest **determent** as they lost meaningful strategic services designed to use tax benefits and savings to increase the probability they could reach their goals on-time and on-budget.

The **current status** of the New School is as the predominate model in the tax services world...a model that simply overpowered the CPAs and the EAs of the Old School. The Old School could not or would not compete with the New School and quickly started to change their business model to mimic that off the New School.

The **reasons for dominance** of the New School over the Old School vary from firm to firm but can be generalized as the New School being more effective, efficient, and more fully satisfies the taxpayer's redirected focus on tax services meaning filing the tax return. Another reason for dominance builds on this redirected focus. Taxpayers began to see tax returns as a commodity and the matrix for selection being cost of preparation. This was not a trend that boded well for the Old School.

A case study in the reasons for dominance of the New School over the Old School is the spectacular rise of H&R Block.

According to their website dated 21 January 2016, H&R Block is the world's largest consumer tax preparation service company and the company that invented the tax preparation category.

In 1955, a juggernaut of a change was launched that eventually blew-out the old school. In 1955, Henry and Richard Block saw an opportunity to market tax preparation (tactical) services only to clients in Kansas City, Missouri. From the recognition of that opportunity, H&R Block became the world-wide financial power it has become.

In my opinion, they changed the face of the profession as they marked the beginning of the separation of strategic and tactical services offered to clients. After seeing the success of H&R Block, similar firms were established.

These H&R Block-type firms overpowered the full-service model for CPAs and EAs, and set the tone professionally and economically for the rise of the New School.

Interesting note...

H&R Block recently recognized the fracture between strategic and tactical services and the void, on a global scale, it left for the small business owner. H&R Block, in the mid-2010s, launched Block Advisors and Block Small Business Services to target the small business market and offer strategic tax and other services to the small business owner.

They were not the only ones to recognize the problems caused to the small business owner by the fracture between strategic and tactical tax services.

The Taxes Mastered School: Full strategic tax services focused on goal achievement

Taxes Mastered was created to provide full strategic tax services focused on goal achievement.

Although our product and service is taxes, we are also a small business. At Taxes Mastered, Inc., we view sound economic decisions as having precedence over tax decisions.

Our standards for internal decision-making process are what we offer to our clients:

- ✓ First Standard: The decision must support achieving goals on-time, on-budget, and with the highest probability of success
- ✓ Second Standard: Use the safest, best, and most prudent paths developed by the tax code to achieve goals
- ✓ Third Standard: Once these two standards are fully satisfied, then the third standard is to make appropriate short-term tax decisions

Taxes Mastered is a **resurrection and adaption** of the Old School: Full Service model updated for the times and to the needs of the small business owner. Resurrection as we offer the full range of strategic services. Adaption as we are very responsive to the technology, backstory, wants, and needs of the small business owner today as we focus on their goal achievement on-time, on-budget, and with the highest probability of success.

Taxes Mastered offers a **high level of personal interaction** and **personal application of the tax code**. We reject commodity-type products and one-answer-fits-all responses. We strongly support the need for custom design and for unique tailoring to specific needs. Our clients want and need the same.

We "buy" things that support, validate, and help achieve our personal goals and values. Our clients want and need the same.

We find purpose and happiness in the achievement of worthy goals. Our clients want and need the same.

We focus on helping clients achieve their goals. Goals are a prime area of personal valuation. Working on goals together shows our acceptance and value towards our clients. Having a focus on achieving their goals is validating to them and deeply rewarding to us.

We serve in the roles of generals and sergeants. We develop strategies to achieve goals on-time, on-budget, and with the highest probability of success. We develop strategies to win the war. We actively assisted with implementation of those strategies. We ensure the reporting of client successes is properly done by New School practitioners of tax preparation.

Our time horizon is before, during, and beyond the current tax year. We start our service for the current tax year in the year preceding. This allows for planning to form an operational model for the year. We stay with the operational model during the year. This allows us to be part of the proactive response to changes that occurred from the anticipated operational model.

We support the tactical efforts of those filing the tax forms. We ensure the reporting accurately and fully reflects the tax strategy adopted as offering the best and safest path to the clients achievement of their goals on-time, on-budget, and with the highest probability of success. We review the reporting to ensure it is a component of our total service of building continually improving models.

We use the tax code in accordance with its highest purpose: to help taxpayers achieve their goals on-time, on-budget, and with the highest probability of success. We understand the primary purpose of the tax code since the mid-1930s is to help taxpayers achieve their goals by offering substantial tax benefits.

We focus on goal achievement; not the tax return. The tax return is a by-product. It is, at best, a third-tier consideration and never of primary importance.

We constantly build What-If scenarios to enhance your probability of achievement. "What-Ifs" is a natural part of our services. As reality unfolds and is gauged against the operational model, reality needs to be reflected. Estimates of the trends and results of reality naturally produce "What-Ifs" as a means of verify the underlying validity of the operational model, and to predict what could happen currently and in the future if various decisions were made

We deliver by using certified professionals. Your Taxes Mastered team contains the professionals needed to develop a strategy to achieve your goals using the safest, best, and most prudent paths provided by the tax code.

We use technology that supports high levels of personal interaction. Technology, properly used, allows us to dramatically increase our one-on-one personal interaction with the client. Technology has its place; however, substituting for personal interaction with clients is not its place.

> *In my opinion*: Our clients are not found in the 85%+ of small business owners that pay too much in tax!

We benefit the client two ways. The first is helping them achieve their goals on-time, on-budget, and with the highest probability of success. The second is replacing fear with peace of mind, uncertainty with stability, and worry with confidence to face the futures.

We are what strategic tax services to small business should be.

Chapter 5: You Pay Too Much In Tax When Goals and Taxing Models Are Not Aligned

Summary

- There are certain goals the tax code wants you to accept.
- Most of these goals are totally compatible with your goals.
- Each goal is assigned to one or more of four taxing models.
- You pay too much in tax when you do not know how to successfully use the four taxing models.

Expanded discussion

The purpose of the tax code is to help you succeed by providing substantial tax savings to achieve specific goals as stated in the tax code. **What are the goals of the tax code?**

As explained in Chapter 3 on the history of the tax code, President Roosevelt and Congress used the concept of social engineering to develop the look and feel for the country they desired. Whether we agree or disagree with the approach, the rightfulness of social engineering, or the goals they established, this is the reality of the tax code faced by the small business owner today…right now. As such, in my opinion, the small business owner should understand the prevalent philosophy of the tax code and learn how to use it to their advantage.

Table 2 lists the major goals supported by the tax code; goals that the tax code wants to see achieved and goals that the tax code will provide substantial tax benefits and savings to the taxpayer as an aid to helping them achieve these goals.

These goals are not listed in any order of relative importance or priority.

Table 2: Major Goals Supported by the Tax Code

Goals supported by the tax code
Providing for surviving spouse
Saving for contingencies
Supplementing retirement
Gifting to family
Gifting to charities
Securing payment of debt
Treating all of your beneficiaries equally
Maximizing ERISA distributions
Increasing current income
Having fun activities now and in the future that for good reasons were delayed
Have an accessible retirement plan only for the business owner

The tax code was engineered to provide material assistance to the taxpayer in achieving these goals. Understanding that all of the goals could not be assisted by the tax code in the same manner, the tax code developed four basic tax models to help you achieve the goals listed in Table 2. These models were based on the economic similarity of the assets within each model and were based on the type of assistance each model provided towards goal achievement.

The first is <u>Model 1</u> and is comprised of your business and real estate. Model 1 is your economic engine. Your business is any economic activity you do with the purpose of making money. For this reason, investment real estate (but not your home) is considered as Model 1.

The second is <u>Model 2</u> and includes your after-tax financial reserves and market investments. Model 2 is basically where most people put the lifestyle income that has not been consumed.

The third is <u>Model 3</u> and is your ERISA and IRA accounts. *ERISA* is an acronym for the Employee Retirement Income Security Act of 1974. A 401(k) plan is an example of a Model 3 ERISA account. *IRA* is an acronym for Individual Retirement Account. While technically not an ERISA plan, an IRA is commonly seen as such due to the overlapping nature of an ERISA plan and an IRA. Please see **Addendum Number 1** at the end of this chapter for a more detailed discussion on ERISA plans. Model 3 ERISA plans and IRAs are generally not a strong tax or economic tool for the small business owner. While wonderful for employees, they rarely meet the needs of the small business employee owner.

The last is <u>Model 4</u> and is your non-qualified plans (NQPs). NQPs are not commonly understood or utilized in the small business owner's tax planning arsenal. Please see **Addendum Number 2** at the end of this chapter for a more detailed description of NQPs. The NQPs lack of use is most unfortunate as they are probably the strongest tax and economic tool in the small business owner's tax arsenal for:

- Sustainable retirement income.

- Increasing current income.
- Providing peace of mind against the uncertainty of market risk.
- Very favorable taxation on earnings of economic assets within the properly constructed NQP: no income taxes on earnings.
- Very favorable taxation on usage of economic assets within the properly constructed NQP: no income taxes on usage.
- Unlimited funding possibilities as opposed to funding restrictions imposed on Model 3.

One of the general reasons small business owners pay too much in tax is due to a great deal of confusion between the primary tax code-target for Model 3 and for Model 4.

In summary, Model 3 is for employees that hold little to none of the equity interest for the business that they work for. Model 3 was established under ERISA, the Employee Retirement Income Security Act of 1974. Please note that the title provided the emphasis of this model: employees. Model 3 is generally not very helpful for small business owners as they strive to reach their goals due to the operational procedures and funding limitations imposed on them by Model 3.

Model 4 are non-qualified plans (NQPs). These are plans that are structured primarily for the small business owner and were designed to meet many of the needs of the small business owner including tax savings, accessibility, and non-uniform contribution amounts.

In structuring Model 4 NQPs, the tax code gave the small business owner the right to:

- Fund their retirement without limits.
- Not to be forced to cover almost all of their employees as is common with a Model 3 ERISA plan.
- Have accessibility to the funds in the plan when they desired and as needed.
- Make unequal and infrequent contributions into the NQPs.

Understanding the difference between Model 3 ERISA plans and Model 4 NQPs is crucial for the small business owner as they avoid paying too much in tax and as they strive to achieve their goals on-time on-budget, and with the highest probability of success.

Table 3 is a comparison of the material characteristics of the Model 3 ERISA plan and the Model 4 NQP.

Table 3: Comparison of Model 3 and Model 4 Taxing Models

Description	Model 3 ERISA plan	Model 4 non-qualified plan
Primary focus	Employee	Small business owner
Limits on annual or total funding	YES	NO
Must include broad-base of all eligible employees	YES	NO
Subject to highly compensated employees (HCS) rules	YES	NO
IRS reporting\filing of a tax return	YES	Generally No
Generally requires a plan administrator	YES	NO
Accessibility before normal retirement age	Generally NO • Very limited exceptions	YES; accessible on day-one if so designed
Tax deduction for contribution	Generally YES	Generally NO although some exceptions exist under the tax code
Tax on growth	YES; paid upon withdrawal	NO
Tax on usage	YES; paid upon withdrawal	NO
Tax on passage of corpus to beneficiaries at death	Generally YES but many exceptions exist	Generally NO but some exceptions exit

However, the tax benefits provided under the tax code for the achievement of its stated goals was not the end of the tax code structure. In addition, the tax code "assigned" the achievement of goals to specific tax models. At times, one goal was satisfied entirely by one model; other times, multiple models were required to satisfy a tax code engineered goals. The tax code provides substantial tax savings when you use these models for what they are intended. Table 4 shows which goal is satisfied by which model.

Table 4: Matching of Goal to Tax Model

Goals supported by the tax code	Primary tax model(s) used to achieve goals
Providing for surviving spouse	Model 2, 4
Saving for contingencies	Model 2 and 4
Supplementing retirement	Model 3 and 4
Gifting to family	Model 1, 2, 3, and 4
Gifting to charities	Model 1, 2, 3, and 4
Securing payment of debt	Model 1, 2, and 4
Treating all of your beneficiaries equally	Model 1, 2, 3 and 4
Maximizing ERISA distributions	Model 3
Increasing current income	Model 1 and 4
Having fun activities now and in the future that for good reasons were delayed	Model 1 (during working years) and Model 4 (during retirement years)
Have an accessible retirement plan only for the business owner	Model 4

Table 4 shows the taxing models selected for goal achievement by the tax code. What do you think your probability of success in reaching your goals on-time and on-budget if you are only using 50% or 75% of the available taxing models? This is why it is important to understand the goals supported by the tax code and their relationship to the taxing models.

In one sense, it is very easy to see if your filed tax return is supporting your goals. There are key lines in the business and personal income tax return that flow into specific models, and specific models flow into achievement of certain goals. Although the following should only be used as a general rule of thumb, given the highly unique nature of each small business income tax return, you can look at your tax return and see your degree of goal achievement.

Table 5 shows the business income tax return lines flowing into each model, and Table 6 shows the personal income tax return lines flowing into each model.

Table 5: Business Income Tax Return Flowing into Specific Models

Description	Tax form page and line with description	Model into which this line flows
Current lifestyle goals	Form 1065\Page 1\Line 9 and 10 Form 1120\Page 1\Line 12 Form 1120S\Page 1\Line 7	Model 1, and 2
Retirement lifestyle, future, and protection goals	Form 1065\Page 1\Line 18 Form 1120\Page 1\Line 26 (included in other deductions) Form 1120S\Page 1\Line 26 (included in other deductions)	Model 3 and Model 4

The tax code is very specific about the organization of the goals. Either the goals are for current lifestyle or the goals are for retirement, future, and protections goals above and beyond current lifestyle.

Another reason that small business owners pay too much in tax is that their major emphasis, as shown by the filing of their tax returns, is towards current lifestyle goals with inadequate attention to retirement lifestyle, future, and protection goals.

Retirement lifestyle, future, and protection goals rarely migrate to the personal income tax return as they are either deductions on the business tax return or are net neutral meaning that the tax effect is zero.

Once the salary leaves the business return, it is reported on the personal income tax return of the small business owner. Salary represents monies consumed for lifestyle.

Excess salary is the monies stored in reserves, usually and most commonly in Model 2. Gain or earnings on these monies is usually taxable and so is reported on the Form 1040 as shown in Table 6.

Table 6: Continued Taxation of Monies Received for Current Lifestyle Goals

Description	Reporting components of salary	Individual income tax form
Salary	Salary	Form 1040\Page 1\Line 7
Excess salary used for reserve purposes	Interest Dividends Capital gains	Form 1040\Page 1\Line 8a Form 1040\Page 1\Line 9a Form 1040\Page 1\Line 13

The tax code provides substantial tax benefits to achieve taxpayer goals selected from Table 2. The amount and timing of the benefit depends upon the unique circumstances of the taxpayer and their ability to structure their business and personal tax affairs to match the four taxing models. One model is not superior to another model in concept. However, one model (or combination of models) is superior to another model in its ability to help the small business owner achieve their goals on-time, on-budget, and with the highest

In my opinion: It is a hard for the typical small business owner, given their experiences with high taxes, to see that today is the time to live and today is the time to fund for tomorrow. Needing to allocate scarce economic resources, their emphasis becomes supporting their current lifestyle, reserving some money for emergencies and expansion in the business, and the payment of taxes.

Tomorrow is not forgotten; while not really funded, it stays in the back of the small business owner's mind as a worry.

This would change if they stopped paying too much in taxes and the future could be appropriately addressed.

probability of success.

One final note…if Model 4 is to provide sufficient retirement lifestyle income, what is the purpose of Model 1 and Model 2 at retirement?

The purpose of Model 1 and Model 2 at retirement is to provide the reserves necessary for the unpredictable.

Model 1 and Model 2 provide the reserves necessary if the "white picket fence blows down" and extensive medical expenses arise, extensive nursing care is needed, or other unpredictable expenses arise; unpredictable as to *When?* and *How Much?* but entirely reasonable and probable. These unpredictable events require additional monies above and beyond normal expenses and lifestyle expenses associated with retirement lifestyle provided by Model 4.

Addendum Number 1: ERISA Plans

Addendum Number 1 explains why Congress invented ERISA, the problems they addressed, and their goal of retirement plan security for participants. It also provides an explanation for my statement that Model 3 ERISA plans are not the best tool, on average, to use for the small business owner as they seek to fund their retirement.

As you can tell from this Addendum, the full intent of Congress was for employee and not owner-employees like the small business owner.

Why Congress Invented ERISA (Employee Retirement Security Income Act of 1974)

Congress invented ERISA to solve problems with previous legislation governing retirement plans. The 1954 Internal Revenue Code was the operable authoritarian standard before ERISA. Congress saw multiple problems with retirement plans operating under the 1954 Internal Revenue Code. These multiple problems caused insufficient focus on the stability of participants' accounts, excessive focus on the compliance of the tax deduction, and an insufficient focus on the self-dealing between the plan sponsor and the plan assets.

The first problem was that the Internal Revenue Service (IRS), as the sole federal compliance agency, received a mandated charge to concentrate on the documentation of contributions into the plan, and not a charge to verify compliance to retirement plan laws or guidelines. When the IRS audited a plan, it did not audit the compliance of the plan to relevant laws, plan asset stability, or composition of plan assets; it audited whether the tax deduction taken by the sponsoring employer equaled the amount paid into the retirement plan.

The second problem was that compliance of retirement plans was at the state level with a conflicting patchwork of rules creating lower standards for employers, and creating hesitancy and uncertainty with regard to rule enforcement. While federal tax requirements were the same for all employers, individual states developed their own rules for plan compliance. The laws of multiple states governed a multistate employer. States would not agree who had primary jurisdiction. This left state regulators unsure how to judge and enforce compliance, and left employers with a tremendous gray area to work within—a gray area causing manipulation of accounts and retirement plan failures of significant numbers to cause concern at the federal level.

The third problem was that there was no primary or secondary focus on the stability of the participants' accounts, since the effective compliance and enforcement focus for retirement plans was at the tax deduction level. The unspoken question never really addressed before ERISA was the stability of the participants' assets: would the money be there as planned, as promised, and as expected when the employee retired?

The fourth problem was that the plans were employer focused. This focus allowed significant economic transactions of dubious nature to occur between sponsors/employers and the retirement plan assets. Sponsors would contribute to the retirement plan, take the tax deduction, and then borrow back the contribution for internal cash flow purposes, leaving the retirement plan with only IOUs based on the good faith of the sponsor. The purpose of pre-ERISA retirement planning legislation was not to create a tax-deductible fund for employer's use, but that is what it became.

Because of these four problems, Congress saw the need for federal oversight, creating uniform rules, and for focusing on the participant. Since the initial adoption of the 1954 Internal Revenue Code, significant problems had occurred causing Congress to desire federal oversight. The acknowledged tipping point for a comprehensive rewrite of pension legislation was the Studebaker bankruptcies.

Studebaker was an automotive manufacturer that failed economically. Studebaker sponsored a retirement plan for its employees that also failed. Because of these bankruptcies, the employees of Studebaker received very little in promised benefits as Studebaker had taken cash from the plan, replaced the cash with IOUs, and then the IOUs proved worthless with the bankruptcy of Studebaker. These IOUs represented the vast majority of plan assets. Studebaker created these IOUs for the company's economic benefit by raising capital not available in the open market in a futile effort to save the company. Studebaker received a tax benefit of lower taxes when funding the contributions into the retirement plan. Studebaker then borrowed back the contributions for internal cash flow purposes, leaving the retirement plan with an IOU dependent on the ability of Studebaker to repay. When employees demanded their benefits from the retirement plan, Studebaker could not repay the IOUs, and the employees could not receive their retirement benefits.

Studebaker was not alone in abusing plan assets and creating mismanagement issues. Jimmy Hoffa, the leader of the International Brotherhood of Teamsters, served four years in prison for a conviction stemming from abusing his union's

Central and Southern States Pension Fund. President Nixon commuted Mr. Hoffa's sentence in 1971. In 1964, Merton Bernstein, a professor at Yale Law School, wrote *The Future of Private Pensions* detailing extensive examples of management abuse and criticizing current retirement plan legislation.

Congress Changes Intent and Focus

The year 1959 saw the enactment of the Welfare and Pension Plans Disclosure Act with substantive amendments in 1962; however, abusive issues continued to occur faster than legislative ability to cope under its current structure. In 1962, President Kennedy appointed the President's Commission on Corporate Pensions that sowed the seeds for regulatory reform. In 1967, Senator Jacob Javits, chairperson of the Senate Labor and Human Resources Committee, introduced bipartisan legislation to correct the documented problems of management abuse of retirement plans. Out of this bipartisan effort, Congress invented ERISA and President Gerald Ford signed it into law on Labor Day of 1974. ERISA took several different focuses than the 1954 Internal Revenue Code.

- *Improving participant confidence.* The federal focus of legislation changed from the employer's tax deductions to the employee's security in receiving the promised/hoped-for benefits. This was a major change in focus.

- *Providing meaningful federal oversight.* Primary jurisdiction was no longer at the state level with standards varying from state to state. Federal oversight was primary and accomplished by joint monitoring of retirement plans by the IRS and the

Department of Labor. With the focus on participants and not sponsors, participants received an expanding freedom of choice. While this book is on the two choices offered to participants for ERISA distributions, other significant areas of choice were in asset selection of plan assets, and in management of plan assets supporting the participants' accounts.

- *Protecting retirement assets from sponsor invasion.* Sponsoring companies could not borrow and then create IOUs with ERISA plan assets. This eliminated the possibility of dubious IOUs, although certain and well-defined ERISA plans could invest solely in employer stock. While the 1954 Internal Revenue Code allowed the predecessor of the indirect distributive option, sponsors could easily nullify this choice, thus keeping liquid assets in the plan—liquid assets they could easily invade.

- *Strengthening the participant's choice to maximize ERISA plan distributions.* Congress wrote provisions into ERISA and into the Internal Revenue Code strengthening the participants' ability to choose the indirect distributive option, maximize ERISA plan distributions, and protect against market loss with reasonable upside gain potential. Although pre-ERISA legislation allowed the sponsor to control employees' distributive options, ERISA places the distributive choice directly in the hands of the participants.

- *Eliminating the effect of market losses coupled with reasonable upside gain potential.* From a perspective of practicality, the result of congressional intent (developing the indirect distributive option, and allowing a CAIUL policy within that option) defined reasonable upside gain potential as 12% to 17% per year. A floor for market loss at 0% eliminated the effect of market losses. Only the indirect distributive option offers this protection and advantage.

- *Reducing fees and penalties.* Fees can be ongoing and once in place can materially erode the net rate of return of plan assets. The legislative goal of Congress was to provide participants with a choice to maximize ERISA distributions; an important aspect of maximizing distributions was allowing participants to choose the lowest cost fee option. Penalties can have the same effect. In the indirect distributive option, penalties usually occur only once instead of a potential multiple times with the direct option. Only in the indirect distributive option can a participant realize the full effect of minimizing fees and penalties.

- *Improving access.* The most common restriction on access to plan assets is age. Congress defined a relatively narrow range of ages where plan assets became accessible without penalty or other financial determent. In the indirect distributive option (but not the direct distributive option), participants can access economic values without a barrier based on age. This was an attempt to match needs of participants with access to retirement plans.

Congress Uses the Internal Revenue Code

To maintain these changes in focus, Congress deeply embedded two options for distributions with differing goals in ERISA legislation and in Internal Revenue Code sections.

The first option was the direct distributive option. The direct option has a primary focus on producing tax revenue for the government. Implementation of this option was a mechanical default. Participants need not take any advanced proactive measures to elect this option; it was a default option with universal applicability. This option focused very successfully on tax revenue production. Due to its default and universal status, this option's taxing methodology resulted in the highest level of taxes paid and no protection of plan assets against the effect of market losses. Its taxing methodology created a tax on each distribution and created the need to keep plan assets in the market fully exposed to market losses. The direct option ensures the taxing of all distributions (as economic transactions). In practical terms, it is an avoidable default if participants were proactive. Chapter 4 analyzes this option.

The second option was the indirect distributive option. This option has a primary focus, due to social engineering within the Internal Revenue Code, on maximizing distributions, full protection of assets from the effect of market losses, and a reasonable upside gain potential. This option fully reflected congressional social intent, and fully achieved its social purpose by all practical and reasonable standards and guides for evaluation. This option, while legislated, becomes effective only on proactive choices made by the participants. Due to its proactive and choice basis, its taxing methodology resulted in the lowest level of taxation and the full protection of plan assets from the effect of market losses with a reasonable upside gain potential. The indirect distributive option has the full authoritarian support of the Internal Revenue Code per the intent of Congress. Congress, through the Internal Revenue Code, wrote this option making the thesis of this book (as stated in Chapter 1) correct. Chapter 5 analyzes this option.

The direct distributive option is the polar-opposite of the indirect distributive option. They are polar-opposites because Congress had two opposite goals (maximizing its tax revenue and maximizing participant's ERISA distributions), and Congress embedded into the Internal Revenue Code full support of each option. Chapter 3 is the background on Congress's use of the Internal Revenue Code to accomplish its purposes.

Addendum Number 2: Non-qualified Plans (NQPs)

(Note: This Addendum is adopted from a book I wrote entitled 5 Essential Tax Strategies for the Contractor. Although addressed to the Contractor, the concepts and conclusions should apply to all small business owners. Therefore, please substitute the term Small Business Owner *for* Contractor *as you read this Addendum.)*

The tax code has differing purposes for qualified and non-qualified plans as part of the safest, quickest, and best path for a Contractor. To truly achieve goals on-time, on-budget, and with the highest probability of success, a Contractor, generally, needs to focus on the non-qualified plan (NQP) with the proper funding and with the proper construction according to the tax code.

Why this concept is important

Money stored for future use is predominately stored within non-qualified plans. These plans have the potential to reduce taxes today and tomorrow.

Expanded discussion

> *Author's note: The key to understanding qualified plans for the Contractor is to remember that they were developed for the employee and not the employer. Therefore, they come with restrictions on funding and accessibility.*
>
> *The key to understanding non-qualified plans (NQP) is they were developed for the employer and allow the employer to fund just for themselves without tax*

code restrictions on funding. Tax deductibility and accessibility vary depending upon the type of NQP selected.

Non-qualified plans

NQPs use long-term funding to build their economic assets for retirement.

Due to the very case-sensitive nature of a non-qualified plan, the IRS has not released a Publication as with ERISA plans; however, the NQPs are well documented in the tax code and were well established by the time of the 1954 IRC.

Due to the wide spectrum of business owner\employees, the tax code gave wide latitude in the design of NQPs; this wide latitude is a prime reason why they are a bedrock tax strategy for the Contractor as well as other classifications of owner\employees. Tax attributes for NQPs also run a wide spectrum as shown in Table 6. There is very little common terminology assigned to NQPs in the tax code or in related professional literature.

Most given names were created by marketing entities promoting certain types of NQPs. Therefore, for Table 6, generic names are used. The percentages are in summary and could change in a specific situation.

The brief summary of NQPs as a concept should not be taken as their having little application in the real tax-world of the Contractor. In fact, quite the opposite is true. However, they are best understood and developed on a case-by-case basis.

The NQP usually more effective for the Contractor *(Note: or small business owner as well)* to reach their goals on-time, on-budget, and with the highest probability of success is the Type D.

The economic corpus of the Type D NQP can only be held in a life insurance product. Because of that, there is a time where accessibility is reduced until the cash surrender values and the accumulated values are equal unless a rider to the policy is purchased to equate the cash surrender value and the accumulated value at the inception of the policy. That ramp-up time until equality varies from product to product but is generally about ten years.

Table 6: Tax Attributes for NQPs

Tax attributes	Type A	Type B	Type C	Type D
Investments	Cash, market investments, annuities, life insurance	Cash, market investments, annuities, life insurance	Cash, market investments, annuities, life insurance	Specifically constructed life insurance
Tax deductibility of contribution	100% after-tax	80% to 90% after-tax with remainder tax deductible	50% to 80% after-tax with remainder tax deductible	30% to 45% after-tax with remainder tax deductible
Tax on growth	Generally yes for market investments; insurance no	Generally yes for market investments; insurance no	Generally yes for market investments; insurance no	Requires insurance as investment; no tax on growth
Tax on usage	Generally yes for market investments; insurance no	Generally yes for market investments; insurance no	Generally yes for market investments; insurance no	Requires insurance as investment; no tax on usage
Tax on passage to beneficiaries at death	Generally yes for market investments; insurance no	Generally yes for market investments; insurance no	Generally yes for market investments; insurance no	Requires insurance as investment; no tax on growth
Retirement funding	Yes	Yes	Yes	Yes
Accessibility	Can be between 0 and 13-years	Can be between 1 and 13 years	Can be between 1 and 13 years	Specifically determined to meet the needs of the Contractor

Discussion on Life Insurance

This section explains whole life insurance (specifically the current assumption indexed universal life insurance policy (IUL) subset of whole life) basics to appreciate why the tax code only allows life insurance to be used in a Type D NQP.

Many people have a narrow view of life insurance, leaving many functions of life insurance off the table. In this narrow view, death benefits are the primary purpose. The economic concern is the ratio of death benefits to premiums paid, since life insurance is expensive and probably something needed but definitely not wanted. If those negatives were not enough, life insurance agents sell the insurance. Sometimes seen as commission driven and not driven by a strong desire to help, they are, however, an essential part of the acquisition process.

Congress had a more expansive view that was legislated into the tax code. Congress historically used life insurance in selected transactions when the goal was maximization of benefits to taxpayers. In Congress's expansive view, the primary purpose of life insurance is the building of tax-free internal values potentially used in the future during lifetime. Death benefits are secondary but provided two benefits: (1) living benefits to fund the cost of catastrophic illness such as terminal illness and critical care (as defined within the life policy) and (2) death benefits required to satisfy the tax code's definition of life insurance. If internal values, or living values, are unused during life, they transfer to the beneficiaries as death benefits with the amount transferred depending on the underlying structure of the policy.

In Congress's expansive view, IUL policies should not be expensive and should have an effective and efficient cost system. This is an emotionally debated point in the economic and financial worlds. In reality, Congress's view can be tested by computing the net benefits received without the NQP and with the NQP with the numeric results compared.

> *Author's comment: It is my position the IUL policy approach produces the highest numeric results in the vast majority of cases. Congress engineered a result using an IUL policy so it would be cost effective and efficient, and produce a high net benefit. It is somewhat pointless to argue the pros and cons of insurance from a theoretical perspective or from the perspective of one or two situations. The best test is a practical application comparing the numerical outcome against other alternatives using reasonable parameters. A reasonable parameter is the effect of market losses. This is why the upcoming discussion on indexing in Chapter 9 is so very interesting.*

All life insurance is either term of whole life; there are no other types. Due to term insurance's actuarial structure, it is not allowable for the indirect distributive option and, therefore, not of use for maximizing ERISA distributions.

Whole life insurance generally, and an IUL policy specifically, has vastly different structural characteristics than term insurance. These are the parties and key structural elements of an IUL policy defined under Internal Revenue Code sections 7702 and 7702a, and supporting authoritarian sources.

- *Insurance company.* The insurance company issues the policy as a reflection of the terms of a contract between the insurance company and the policy owner. The insurance company issuing the policy is compliant or noncompliant with Internal Revenue Code sections 7702 and 7702a. The insurance company is responsible for the existence of living and death benefits per the contract, subject to premiums paid by the owner.

- *Premiums.* These are the agreed-to payments made by the owner to the insurance company under the terms and conditions of the insurance policy. The policy determines the amount, frequency, and duration of the premiums. It is not always necessary to pay premiums for the whole life of the insured, even though the benefits of the policy are for the whole life.

- *Insured.* The insured is the individual whose life governs the costs of the policy and, when deceased, the payment of the death benefit. With whole life in general, one or multiple lives can be the insured.
- Regardless of the number of insureds, each insured must be an individual human being.

- *Costs.* Insurance costs computed for the whole life of the insured include sufficient amounts for the build-up of internal values and the death benefit payable at the insured's demise. Costs are reflective of many factors, including insurance, health, age, and gender. Costs are also reflective of the ratio between death benefits and the build-up of internal values. The structure of the policy, the relationship of death benefits to living benefits, and the projected need of withdrawals from the living benefits requires much thought. This thought process is the core rationalization for the need for the life insurance Contractor.

- *Owner.* The party, individual, or entity who enjoys all of the incidents of ownership, including access to living values, ability to change beneficiaries, and to modify the policy in negotiation with the insurance company is considered the owner. The owner pays the premium.

- *Beneficiaries.* The beneficiaries will receive the death benefit upon the demise of the insured. They can be individuals, entities, or a combination of both. The beneficiaries can be one or multiple parties.

- *Usefulness.* A whole life policy generally increases its usefulness over time due to the build-up in internal values (living benefits).

- *Marketing types of whole life.* Marketing departments have developed many names for their particular variation of whole life, but all whole life, regardless of marketing terminology, rides on the chassis structured under Internal Revenue Code sections 7702 and 7702a. Some common marketing terminology for these whole life policies include whole life, universal life, equity universal life, indexed universal life, IUL policy, and variable universal life.

- *IUL.* IUL policies are a specific subset of whole life. An IUL is the policy used for the case study since this author believes it is the most compliant to the engineering intent of Congress and most compliant with the requirements of Internal Revenue Code sections 7702 and 7702a for Contractors. Therefore, the thesis and its supporting arguments throughout this book reflect an IUL policy. The thesis of this book might not be true if based on a non-IUL whole life product.

- *Guarantee against market loss.* (See Chapter 9 for an expanded discussion on guarantees against market losses called *Indexing.*) An IUL policy contractually ties the growth rate of its accumulated values to an independent index of general availability. Commonly, the index is the S&P 500, although other indexes are available. The S&P 500, by itself, has no limit on losses (downside) and no limits on its gains (upside). However, the IUL policy contractually guarantees a modification to the index's downside and upside economic consequences. In an IUL policy, downside is limited to a floor of 0% generally with an upside ceiling of 12% to 17%, depending on the policy chosen.

These parties and key structural elements set the platform for the favorable tax methodology given to IUL policies. The favorable taxing methodology is from the tax code classifying so many key and positive benefits as tax-free.

Taxing Methodology of an IUL POLICY

In the tax world, monies are either tax inefficient (after-tax dollars) or tax efficient (pretax dollars to varying degrees). After premiums are flowed into the policy, the life policy has a very favorable tax methodology as summarized in Figure 2.

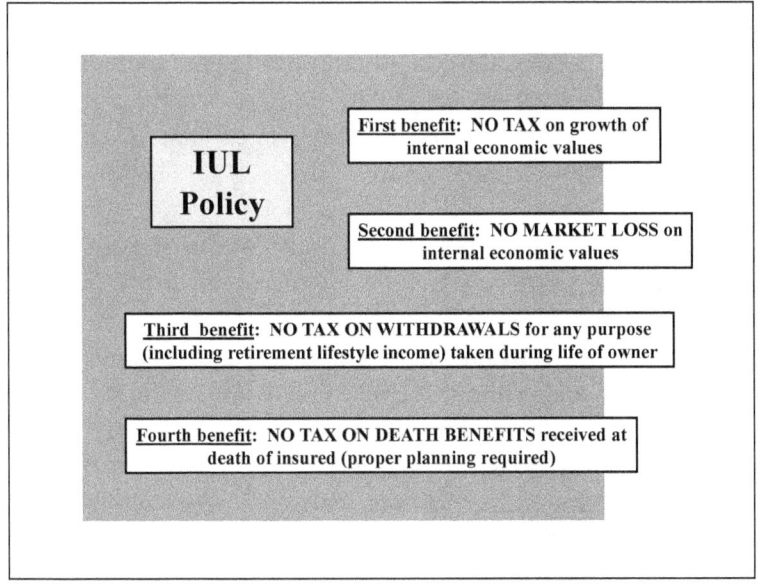

Figure 2: Taxing Methodology of a IUL Policy.

There are four powerful benefits provided by the several favorable effects of taxing methodology. The first benefit is there is no tax on growth of internal economic values. Economic values inside the policy grow tax-free; the tax load does not reduce the economic growth rate. This improves the net rate of return and allows the internal economic assets to grow faster, all other factors being equal.

The second benefit is there is no market loss on internal economic values. *Indexing* is the tax strategy eliminating the effect of market losses inside an IUL policy. An indexed policy means the economic growth rate is indexed (referenced by attachment although not necessarily actual investment) to an outside standard and grows with that standard. It does not diminish should that index suffer

60

market losses. The most common index for IUL policies is the S&P 500. If the S&P 500 suffers a loss, that loss does not affect the economic values inside the IUL policy. If the S&P 500 has a gain, the full amount of the gain increases the value of the IUL policy subject to the 12% or 17% ceiling. *(Note: See Chapter 6 in this book for an expanded discussion on Indexing.)*

The third benefit is no tax on withdrawals from the IUL policy for any purpose (including withdrawals for retirement lifestyle income) taken during the life of the owner. The participant\owner withdraws retirement lifestyle money when needed and without restrictions on access due to age-related penalties. There is no tax on the withdrawal. If the participant wants $100, the participant takes $100, and no money is due for taxes. Withdrawals are at the needs and wants of the participant and not within the age ranges established by the government.

The fourth benefit is there is no tax on death benefits received at death of insured. With proper planning, beneficiaries receive the death benefits tax free without a dilution for taxes. Effectively, 100% of death benefits go for their intended purposes.

Benefit Numbers 1, 3, and 4 are available with all whole life policies. Benefit Number 2 (no market loss) is specific to IUL policy and achieved through indexing. Indexing establishes a floor for losses and a ceiling for reasonable upside growth potential; economic values can only fluctuate between the floor and the ceiling. Loss cannot go below the floor, and gains cannot pass through the ceiling. As a practical matter for the indirect distributive option, the floor loss is 0%, and the gain ceiling is between 12% and 17% per year.

When Congress developed the IUL, balance was sought between accessibility and tax advantages. Figure 3 outlines the general relationship between accessibility and tax advantages. In general, as the need for accessibility for increases, the amount of immediate tax advantages decrease.

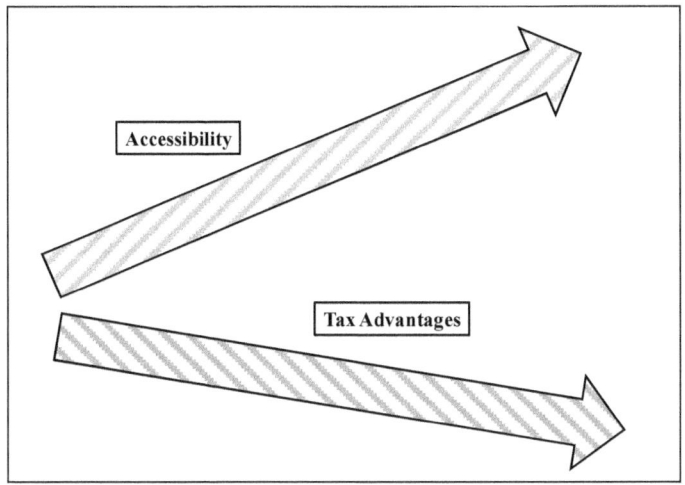

Figure 3: General Relationship between Accessibility and Tax Advantages.

If full accessibility per the terms of the annuity or life insurance contract is acceptable at ten years or so, there is no need to accelerate the accessibility.

If ten years is too long to delay full accessibility, there is a positive and prudent action that can be taken to shorten the distance between accessibility and tax advantages. The action is to purchase a rider on the policy allowing cash surrender value and accumulated value to equal each other anytime from the inception of the policy to the date of "normal" equality commonly at the tenth anniversary of the policy. This acceleration of equating cash surrender value to accumulated value before the typical time of about ten years (depending upon the specifics of the policy selected) is called a "bump-up".

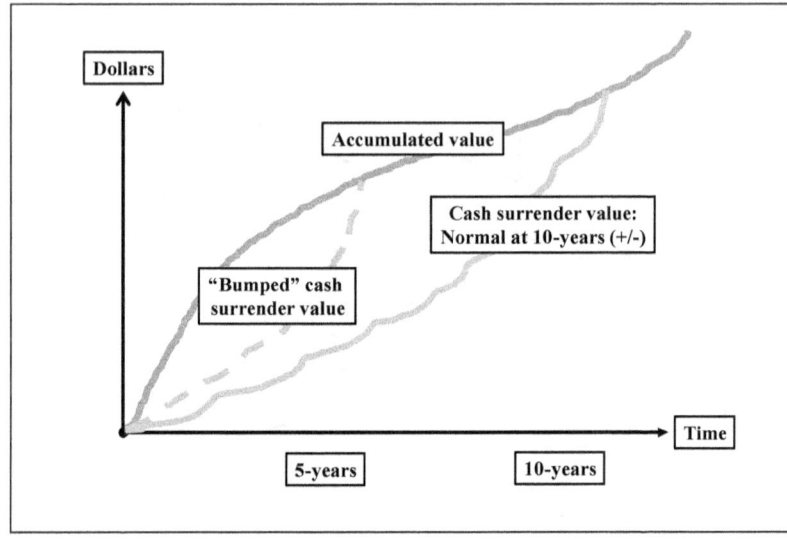

Figure 4: "Bumping-up" the Curve

Economic values generally assessable within a life insurance policy are based on the cash surrender value. A goal for accessibility within a life insurance policy is to have cash surrender value equal accumulated value as this maximizes the accessibility of economic values within the policy. When you "bump-up" the curve (as shown by the dotted line), you are decreasing the time it takes for full access of the economic value within the policy, per the terms of the policy, from generally 10-years to something less. 5-years is common in practice. Therefore, total access comes in 5-years as a general rule.

This "bump-up" is done within the design of the policy, and must be done in cooperation with the issuing insurance company.

Attention should be given to the effect of the bump on accumulated value to ensure it is not impaired. While there is a slow-down in the rate of growth of the accumulated value caused by the cost of the rider for the bump, it is generally not material to the resultant cash distributions from the policy depending upon their date to the date of inception of the policy.

Chapter 6: You Pay Too Much In Tax When You Drive Risk from Reasonable to Beyond

Summary

- The tax code understands acceptance of the wrong levels of risk can destroy your ability to achieve your goals.
- The tax code wants you to succeed.
- The tax code allocates differing levels of risk (risk tolerances) to each of the four taxing models in line with their purpose.
- You pay too much in tax when you mismatch risk levels to its respective model tolerances.

Expanded discussion

Risk is defined many ways in a great variety of situations. For the purpose of our discussion, and as given in the definitions section, *risk* is defined as:

- A situation exposed to danger.
- Probability of a loss or drop in value.
- Reflects the uncertainty of expected gain.
- Means you can lose some or all of your investment.
- Creates uncertainty and threatens peace of mind.
- Creates the opportunity of positive gain.
- Necessary to earn an economic reward.

Each of the four taxing models was structured by the tax code to accept differing levels of risk based on the goals that model was meant to help achieve. Therefore, the tax code does not expect or even promote the idea of having the same level of risk in economic assets held in each of the four taxing models.

Table 7 summarizes the tax code's match of risk levels to its respective model tolerances.

Table 7: Matching of Risk Levels to Taxing Model Tolerances

Taxing Model	Tax code's matching of risk level to tax model tolerances
Model 1	Exposure to unlimited risk; no ceiling on potential gain and no floor on potential loss
Model 2	Exposure to unlimited risk; no ceiling on potential gain and no floor on potential loss
Model 3	Subclass 1: Exposure to unlimited risk; no ceiling on potential gain and no floor on potential loss (minimal) Subclass 2: Exposure to limited risk; ceiling on potential gains and 0% floor on potential losses (major emphasis)
Model 4	Exposure to limited risk; ceiling on potential gains and 0% floor on potential losses

Model 3 has two subclasses as the tax code thought some limited exposure to market loss was acceptable; however, the tax code's goal was to preserve corpus from loss.

Why would the tax code care about risk?

Risk reflects the tax code's primary focus for the four models.

Model 1 and Model 2 were primarily current lifestyle models with most of the economic assets being consumed in lifestyle. Therefore, uncontrolled risk was more acceptable in Model 1 and Model 2. In addition, the tax code thought that the reserves from current lifestyle would be minimal as it anticipated that the amount flowing into Model 1 and Model 2 would be enough for current lifestyle, tax on that lifestyle, and a minor amount for reserves.

The major social engineering purpose of Model 3 and 4 is to provide a certain and stable base for retirement and future needs thus creating peace of mind and confidence in the taxpayer as they age into their retirement lifestyle period. Therefore, the tax code sought to control risk levels in Model 3 and Model 4.

Model 3 and 4 involves a long-term funding commitment made during the same time period as funding for current lifestyle occurs. Long-term funding was the key; little now for sufficient later. Replacement of corpus is difficult if not impossible, from a practical perspective, after certain ages are reached given the long-term nature of funding.

Risk, by one definition, involves loss to corpus from market performance. Destruction of corpus from market swings is to be avoided. When market goes below 0%, this can destroy years and years of gain in a very short time period. Therefore, tax code limits risk to 0% loss as a floor and 12% to 17% gain as a ceiling.

Risk, by another definition, involves loss to corpus from tax loads. Tax loads slow-down the growth of the Model 3 and Model 4 taxing models. The tax code deemed the social purpose of a certain, stable, and peace of mind generating retirement plan to be so important that taxes were basically eliminated. Therefore, it created a preferred risk model with these major elements:

- No tax on growth
- No tax on usage
- No tax when corpus, with proper planning, is passed to designated beneficiaries upon the death of the SBO.
- Economic performance tied to an outside, wide-based, and commonly accepted standard; the S&P 500 is the most commonly accepted standards for this purpose.

Indexing is the mechanism created by the tax code to control risk to what it deemed as acceptable levels.

Indexing is a tax and economic concept that incorporates no taxes on growth, no taxes on usage, economic performance tied to an outside standard, and the use of a ceiling and a floor to control risk. Indexing was created by the tax code to protect the economic assets held in Model 3 and Model 4, and to provide a high degree of certainty and confidence in the future for the small business owner as they age into retirement.

While used in Model 3 and Model 4, the most common use of indexing for the small business owner is in Model 4 non-qualified plans (NQPs).

As a further explanation of indexing, the following is adopted from an article I wrote on indexing as it applies to Model 4 NQPs. I wrote the article as part of a series on the use of Model 4 NQPs for small business owners explaining why this was such an important tool in achieving their goals. In following up with readers who had completed the series of articles, I learned there were many points of similarity in how they viewed NQPs.

- ✓ NQPs were a logical place to start with retirement funding.
- ✓ NQPs eliminated the problems they were having in funding their own retirement through a Model 3 ERISA plan.
- ✓ NQPs used a lower contribution-longer funding period that fit in nicely with their cash flow.
- ✓ NQPs economic assets had a far greater ease of accessibility than Model 3 ERISA plans.
- ✓ NQPs allowed them to achieve many goals by using the same contribution dollar. For example, the death benefit (if properly constructed) allowed for providing of economic protection for the spouse as well as a source for long-term care, as an example. No longer did they have the need to purchase death benefit and long-term care as separate items.

(Start of article)

Economic depletion due to market loss is a very real and a very fatal consideration. However, eliminating market loss without provide for a reasonable expectation of market gain at a 12% to 17% ceiling per year is not prudent. The concept of indexing allows for a contractual guarantee against market loss with an upside gain potential ceiling of 12% to 17% per year.

Indexing is treated as a concept; however, it is so important it almost rises to the level of a strategy.

Why this concept is important

Indexing is only allowed by the tax code for specifically designed annuities and life insurance.

When an taxpayer hears annuities and life insurance, generally the first reaction is to reject these investment vehicles as too expensive, too slow to grow, and too "old school" to be a material part of their safe path.

> *Author's Comment: In reality, this is a wrong thought and a material reason most taxpayers do not reach their goals on-time, on-budget, and with the highest probability of success.*
>
> *Why? In my experience as a CPA, RIA, developer of mathematical predictive models, and consultant, I will make this conclusion: subjecting capital to the full impact of market loss has destroyed more portfolios than unlimited market gain has saved. In my experience, market investments subject to full market loss have grown at a slower rate than indexed investment products.*
>
> *If you want to increase your probability of success in reaching your goals, using the tax code concept of indexing is an important marker along your safe path.*

Indexing is not the same as an indexed mutual fund

Indexing within a life insurance policy or within an annuity contract is not the same as an indexed mutual fund.

An indexed mutual fund has growth tied to an independent index like the S&P 500 (similarity) but commonly addresses market loss through portfolio diversity without offering a written guarantee against the effect of market loss on investment assets (difference). In an indexed mutual fund, losses can go below the indexed life insurance policy or annuity floor of 0% as the lowest rate of return possible (difference), and gains can go above the indexed insurance policy or annuity contract ceiling of 12% to 17% (difference).

For clarification of the following discussion on indexing, the S&P 500 calculated without using indexing is termed the *raw S&P 500* while the S&P 500 using indexing is termed the *index S&P 500*. The general features of indexing within a life insurance policy are as follows. While annuity contracts have differing terminology and terms and conditions, in theoretical concept, indexing functions much like indexing within a life insurance contract.

- Growth rate for a life insurance policy is set to an independent standard called an index. The index is independent and based on an outside, objective standard the insurance company cannot control. The most common index is the S&P 500, although others are available. Non-indexed life insurance policies generally have a growth rate commonly set at arbitrary standards established by the insurance company, even if the growth rate is somewhat referenced to an independent standard.
- Growth rate has a loss floor. Under an indexed life insurance policy, the floor is set at 0%, meaning no matter what loss the index takes, the loss suffered by the economic assets within the life insurance policy is set at the floor of 0%. This controls the effect of market losses. Some indexed life insurance policies have a floor greater than 0%.

- Growth rate has a ceiling. In exchange for accepting the floor and the safety of eliminating the effect of market losses on the assets, indexed life insurance policies have a ceiling on the maximum amount of gain enjoyed by the assets. While this ceiling varies by insurance company and by policy within a company, a range of 12% to 17% is common.
- An associated concept to ceilings and floors is the participation percentage. The participation rate defines the percentage of participation in various elements of the indexed life insurance policy. For example, if the ceiling is 12% and the participation rate is 50%, then the ceiling is actually 6% (12% × 50%). The participation rate used in this Library Article is 100%.

The following example of indexing uses the S&P 500 for a ten-year period from 1973 to 1982. Before proceeding with the example, some explanations are required. The purpose of the example is to illustrate that control of losses can maximize and stabilize asset balances. Readers should select their own parameters, run the mathematics (as outlined below) and see if they support the conclusion about the beneficial nature of controlling loss.

> *Author's comment: I believe in any meaningful selection of a time period for the S&P 500, with very few notable exceptions limited as to their time period, the conclusion will be the same as given in Table 1 and Figure15, although the beneficial amount will differ.*
>
> *Indexing is a concept used for social engineering purposes and has uses in many other safest, quickest, and best paths established by the tax code so*

taxpayers can achieve their goals on-time, on-budget, and with the highest probability of success.

There is nothing magical about a ten-year period. A ten-year period is long enough to show trends and movement but not so long that the educational value is lost. Readers can select their own length as they run a test model but should ensure it is of sufficient length to make a valid model.

There is nothing magical about the years selected. Using earlier years of the S&P 500 rather than later removes any emotional reaction by the reader toward the loss and treats the loss as a historical matter. Indexing cannot be used for the management of stocks, mutual funds, or other similar investment options as there cannot be a written guarantee provided by the issuer of those investment options. Therefore, while not a universal concept, indexing is a concept that can work very well within the parameters of its use as provided by the tax code.

Table 1: Data Used to Compare Indexed S&P 500 to Raw S&P 500

End of Year	Raw S&P 500 Growth Rate	Balance	Indexed S&P 500 Ceiling and Floor Rates	Balance
Start balance		10,000		10,000
1973	-18.83%	8,117	0.00%	10,000
1974	-28.36%	5,815	0.00%	10,000
1975	31.38%	7,640	12.00%	11,200
1976	19.15%	9,103	12.00%	12,544
1977	-11.50%	8,056	0.00%	12,544
1978	-6.15%	7,561	0.00%	12,544
1979	7.69%	8,142	7.69%	13,509
1980	12.31%	9,144	12.00%	15,130
1981	25.77%	11,501	12.00%	16,945
1982	-9.73%	**10,382**	0.00%	**16,945**

Source: Extracted from Yahoo finance\History of S&P 500

Using the data from Table 1, the S&P 500 balance (subject to the full effect of market gains and losses) and the Indexing balance (controlling the effect of market losses and limiting the upside gain potential) results in the graph shown in Figure 5.

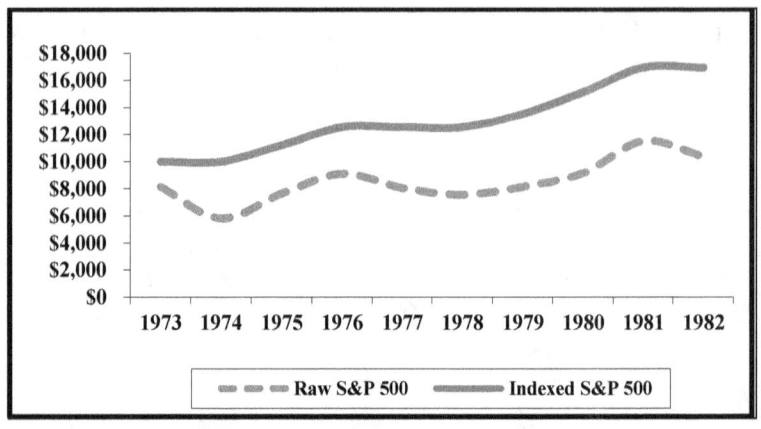

Figure 1: S&P 500 Comparison 1973 to 1982.

In this example, the indexing example with a 0% floor on losses and a 12% to the full effect of gains and losses, the raw S&P 500 grew to $10,382 while the indexed S&P 500 grew to $16,945.

The indexed S&P 500 outperformed the raw S&P 500 by $6,564 ($16,945 – $10,382) or 63.24% ($6,564/$10,380). This is a substantial difference. This example needs caution in its application. It is mathematically possible to find a few selected periods where the raw S&P 500 had greater performance than the indexed S&P 500. Management of economic values for retirement lifestyle income needs more than a few selected years. Rather, management of economic values needs long-term analysis.

> *Author's comment: My opinion is long-term analysis solidly justifies the indexed approach for maximizing yields over time as having a higher probability of success than the raw approach due to the elimination of market losses yet still allowing for a reasonable upside gain potential.*

> *Yet, do I have all of my personal funds under an index philosophy? The answer is No. I believe a blend between indexing and non-indexing approaches are needed. This blend is consistent with the four tax models developed in the tax code (Internal Revenue Code of 1986), their uses, and how they were structured to achieve goals of the taxpayer. The problem becomes, as is almost always the case, when indexing or non-indexing comprises an unhealthy portion of your total asset management approach.* **However, taxing Model 4, generally speaking, should always be based on indexing.**

Congress felt this substantial difference could be typical of participants' experiences over time.

Congress felt indexing would preserve higher values (thereby increasing the base for distributions) and protecting distributions coming from a down period (a distribution taken when the assets had been diminished due to market losses).

Congress felt indexing was an essential component of the total approach for the Contractor, and an essential component in maximizing distributions and protecting assets from the effect of market losses.

(End of article)

Indexing can apply to Model 3. However, the tax code views Model 3 as retirement funding for employees and not the small business owner-employee. Model 3 is created by the Employee Income Retirement Security Act (ERISA) of 1974 as discussed earlier. Model 3 is generally not very useful for small business owners. Indexing is fully applied as standard within Model 4.

Chapter 7: You Pay Too Much In Tax When You Do Not Know Your End Game

Summary

- *The tax code primary purpose is to help taxpayers achieve specific, tax code-approve goals.*
- *How could you achieve unless you knew the end goals (end game)?*
- *You will pay too much in tax if your end game is not well developed.*
- *You will pay too much in tax if your end game is not the focus of your activities.*

Expanded discussion

It might seem odd to some readers that a tax book would have as the final reason small business owners pay too much in tax is that their end game is poorly defined, if defined at all, or that their end game is not the focus of their activities.

The tax code is driven by goals and by the achievement of those goals. The tax code believes that the small business owner is driven by goals and by the achievement of those goals. This is why the tax code thought that this sharing of goal driven philosophy would make social engineering acceptable to the small business owner and a beneficial tool they would readily adopt and embrace.

Retirement is the chief and favored goal of the tax code. **Why? Retirement is the end game.**

The tax code believes that if the end game is won, then the other activities, as a whole, were performed well and integrated into the overall plan. Retirement is the ultimate focus of all activities that make up Model 1 and Model 2. Model 3 is also a focus of retirement. It is just not the right model for the small business owner.

Economic activities build to achievement at retirement. Successful retirement means that all interim goals have been achieved. Retirement is having:
- Sufficient cash flow.
- Sufficient reserves.
- Peace of mind and certainty off occurrence as the small business owner enjoys the last cycle of their life.

If the end game is not known, how can it be achieved? If peace of mind is the goal and it is not reached, will fear and uncertainty about the future take its place?

This is shown by the taxing models. Unless Model 4 is present and fully functional for the small business owner, just using Models 1, 2, and 3 can result in very high tax loads and totally uncontrollable market risk over a long period of time and can result in fear and uncertainty about the future. Risk is allowed to run uncontrolled with uncertainty of financial stability the result.

Systematic planning and funding for retirement by using the proper balance of the four taxing models within the proper time period saves taxes and offers a higher probability of reaching your goals on-time and on-budget.

The tax code breaks-down the end game into three components.

The first is the age you wish to retire. This is important as it defines the number of years you need to have sufficient retirement lifestyle income. It sets the guidelines for the funding period.

The second is the after-tax, and relatively certain, amount you wish to have during those retirement years. This is usually expressed in current dollars meaning the dollars you would need today.

The third is the amount of cash you wish to have on-hand and fully accessible within 5 days at the date of your retirement. For ease of calculation, this age is generally defined as age 65 but needs to be refined based on the unique circumstances of the small business owner.

Once those three components are known, and of course they may change over time, then Model 4 can be properly constructed. Until those three components are known, the end game is uncertain and the future tentative.

Your end game is funded by the performance of your economic engines in Model 1 predominately and by the avoidance of paying too much in tax. The tax code encourages you to achieve by offering tax benefits that produce tax savings.

Tax savings is a term used very loosely. In the tax code, tax savings are divided into groups distinguished by time and the nature of the economic asset discussed:

- ✓ Taxes for the current year's tax return.
- ✓ Taxes based on economic growth from today forward.

- ✓ Taxes based on usage of economic resources from today forward.

The term *tax savings* is reflective of all three divisions of taxes by time and by nature of the economic asset discussed. When I use the term *tax savings*, I am referring to the strategic and tactic operations necessary to secure tax benefits in all three classifications and the total of monies saved from all three classifications.

You will pay too much in tax when your end game is not aligned to the proper strategy for tax savings.

Chapter 8: An Easy Way to Know if You Pay Too Much in Taxes

Is there an easy way to determine if you are paying too much in tax? To determine if you are one of the many small business owners in the 85%+ category that are paying too much in taxes?

The answer is a resounding YES!

The background for the answer to this question goes back to the time mentioned in *Chapter 1: From Being Dismissive to Believing*. After believing, I began to gather client and non-client stories as to why they thought they paid too much in taxes, I interviewed other tax professionals, I sent out assessments, and in other ways gathered appropriate data to (1) determine if small business owner's statement that they paid too much in taxes was true and (2) if so, what was the reasons?

The results?

Result number 1 is I determined that 85%+ of all small business owners pay too much in tax.

Result number 2 is I determined the core reasons they paid too much in tax. These core reasons are the chapters in this book.

Result Number 3 is I developed a simple assessment that was very accurate in determining if a small business owner did, in fact, pay too much in tax. That assessment takes less than 5-minutes, on average, to complete and can be found on Taxes Mastered website at www.TaxesMastered.com.

At the end of the assessment, you will immediately receive a score. Based on that score, you will know if you are paying too much in tax.

Why the score is not definitive, it does provide a very accurate picture for the small business owner. The lower the percentage provided at the end of the assessment, the higher the probability (and the higher the amount) that they are paying too much in taxes. The higher the percentage, the higher the probability they are using the tax code to their benefit and paying just their fair share. It is not realistic to assume you can pay less than your fair share of taxes while enjoying all of the benefits the tax code offers in a safe, prudent, and mature manner.

Within a few days after taking the assessment, you will also receive two reports from Taxes Mastered.

The first report is a copy of your assessment responses plus the *Highest Probability of Success Answers* for that question as given by the tax code. These are answers to the questions that the tax code would deem as giving to the taxpayer the highest amount of tax benefits, the lowest overall amount of taxes paid, and the highest probability in achieving their goals on-time and on-budget.

The second report is a generalized summary of your assessment results as determined by the tax team at Taxes Mastered. This provides a general feel for areas that are problematic and strongly contributing to you paying too much in tax, if that is the result of the assessment.

I invite you to take this assessment and determine if you are paying too much in taxes and, if so, the general reason for that overpayment. All you have to lose is your overly high tax load burden; what you have to gain is to achieve your goals on-time on-budget, and with the highest probability of success using the safe and prudent paths of the tax code.

Chapter 9: Definitions

In the book, I use terms that might not be generally understood by the reader as I might be using them in a technical sense and they are reading in a general or street-sense. I offer these definitions in a hope that they clarify certain of the discussions in the book.

A-J

- *Blaming the messenger* is when the deliverer of bad news is treated as the sole reason for the bad news delivered. Thus, if the messenger is killed, the bad news no longer exists. Expressed by Sophocles in his play *Antigone* where the tyrant Oedipus 'killed' messengers for conveying bad news. Expressed by Shakespeare in *Henry IV, Part II* and in *Antony and Cleopatra.*
- *Certified Public Accountant (CPA)* is a license granted by the state based on educational training, suitable performance on a multi-day examination, and acceptance of a rigorous ethics canon. Taxes are a focus of the CPA examination. Continued professional education is mandated to continue practicing as a CPA. The CPA license was first offered in New York State on 17 April 1896.
- *Enrolled Agent (EA)* is a federal license and represents the highest credentials awarded by the Internal Revenue Service. The EA license is granted after successfully completing a three-part comprehensive IRS test, or through experiences as a former IRS employee, and acceptance of a rigorous ethics canon. Continued professional education is mandated to continue practice as an EA. The history

of the EA license can be traced to approximately 1884.
- *Indexing* is a tax and economic concept that incorporates no taxes on growth, no taxes on usage, economic performance tied to an outside standard, and the use of a ceiling and a floor to control risk.
- *Internal Revenue Code of 1986 (tax code)* is the domestic portion of federal tax law as published in various volumes. It implementing agency is the Internal Revenue Service (IRS).
- *Internal Revenue Service (IRS)* is the governmental agency charged with the collection of taxes and the administering of the Internal Revenue Code of 1986.

K-T

- *The progressive theory* is a philosophy that bands taxable income into ranges with each increasing range taxed at a higher rate per taxable dollar than the previous range.
- *Reward* reflects the promise of economic positive gain
  - Means you will increase the economic amount of your investment
  - Creates peace of mind
  - Necessary to achieve your goals
  - Generally, directly related to risk
  - Higher the risk, the greater the reward. This is not always a true relationship.
- *Risk*
  - A situation exposed to danger
  - Probability of a loss or drop in value
  - Reflects the uncertainty of expected gain.
  - Means you can lose some, or all of your investment

- o Creates uncertainty and threatens peace of mind.
- o Creates the opportunity of positive gain
- o Necessary to earn an economic reward
- *Social engineering* is the process where Congress established goals within the tax code they felt were in the best interest of the country. To encourage taxpayers to accept these goals, the tax code offered substantial tax benefits to complying taxpayers. Another name for *social engineering* is developing safe and prudent paths within the tax code so complying taxpayers could receive substantial tax benefits to achieve their goals on-time, on-budget, and with the highest probability of success.
- *Strategy* or *strategic* is the development of a plan of action towards the achievement of a specific and workable goal; achievement defined within a specific time period. The plan, for the purpose of this book, must be supportable by adherence to the authoritarian standard of the tax code. *Strategy* is the overall plan developed for execution. In strategy, great ideas to use the tax code to accelerate the achievement of goals for the client are developed and detailed plans for implementation are drawn. *Strategy*, in one sense, is what to do, how to do it, and why it is being done. Another explanation is implementing good ideas that greatly help a client achieve their goals
- *Tax code* refers to the Internal Revenue Code of 1986 (IRC). The IRC is the domestic federal tax law in the United States and identified as Title 26 of the United States Code (USC).
- *Tactical* is the implementation of the strategy. Tactical, in one sense, is getting it done. Another explanation is preparing a tax return.

- *Tax planning* is the strategic development of a tax plan and ensuring all of the parts function harmoniously as a combine whole.
- *Tax Preparer* can be a CPA, EA, or someone working part-time with minimal formal or practical education on the tax code. Regardless of background or license standing, their role is the same: document your compliance with the tax code requirements through the filing of forms.
- *Tax preparing* is a tactic documentation of the strategic plan against the standards of the tax code by reporting the economic transactions on the appropriate tax form.
- *Tax savings* in the tax code are divided into groups distinguished by time: (1) taxes for the current year's tax return, (2) taxes based on economic growth from today forward, and (3) taxes based on usage of economic resources from today forward. The term *tax savings* is reflective of all three divisions of taxes by timeframes.

U-Z

- No definitions offered

Disclosures and Disclaimers

In the world we live in today, I am required to list the disclosures and disclaimers associated with this book on a summary level.

John C. Brooke is the author of this book and is based on his experiences, background, understanding of events he was a part of, and his opinion of those experiences and events based on his understanding of the Internal Revenue Code of 1986 (tax code). This book copyrighted and published by Taxes Mastered, Inc. For contact information for Mr. Brooke and Taxes Mastered, Inc. please go to www.TaxesMastered.com.

Representations: Nothing in this communication or attachments, if any, rises to the level of a representation.

The IRS requires John C. Brooke and Taxes Mastered, Inc. to advise you, the reader, that any federal tax advice contained in a memorandum or attachments, if any, is not intended to be used and cannot be used, for the purpose of avoiding penalties under the Internal Revenue Code or for promoting, marketing, or recommending to another party any transaction or matter addressed herein.

This book may contain numeric, graphic or narrative presentations that are theoretical in nature and provided only for educational and exploratory purposes. Only third parties to John C. Brooke and Taxes Mastered, Inc. provide non-theoretical presentations and representations.

© **Copyright** 2017 by Taxes Mastered, Inc.

Finally, although I believe this book to be well-researched and the conclusions very supportable, reread *Friendly Word* *of Advice* and remember…please do not implement any of the concepts or ideas discussed or recommended in this book without appropriate and full assistance from a Certified Taxes Mastered Team Member. Please contact Taxes Mastered, Inc. for a list of Certified Team Members in your area.

www.ingramcontent.com/pod-product-compliance
Lightning Source LLC
Chambersburg PA
CBHW070311230526
45470CB00002B/814